Computer Wings

Diagram Maker

Course Book

Syllabus Version 1.0

First Edition 2009

ISBN 9780 7517 5756 9

British Library Cataloguing-in-Publication Data
A catalogue record for this book is available from the British
Library

A joint publication from:

Q-Validus Ltd.

NovaUCD   t: + 353 1 716 3742
Belfield   e: info@computerwings.com
Innovation Park   w: www.computerwings.com
University College Dublin   w: www.q-validus.com
Dublin 4
Ireland

BPP Learning Media Ltd.

BPP House, Aldine Place   t: 0845 0751 100 (within the UK)
London W12 8AA   t: + 44 (0) 20 8740 2211
United Kingdom   e: learningmedia@bpp.com
                                w: www.bpp.com/learningmedia

Computer Wings® is a registered trademark of Q-Validus Limited in Ireland and other countries. This Computer Wings approved training material may be used in assisting candidates to prepare for their Computer Wings certification test.

Candidates wishing to sit Computer Wings certification tests are required to pre-register for the programme. Candidates may register at any Authorised Centre.

Without registration no certification tests can be taken and no Computer Wings certificate or any other form of recognition may be awarded.

For any further information about Computer Wings visit www.computerwings.com

CONTENTS

What is Computer Wings?

Computer Wings is an exciting new practical computer skills certification programme for real world tasks and roles in the modern workplace.

The certification delivers knowledge and skills in a range of areas. The Computer Wings programme assists candidates to achieve increased efficiency, higher standards of output, and greater levels of collaboration and improved user confidence.

The Computer Wings programme covers the key functions within an organisation such as planning, project management, communication, marketing, IT, online business and process flows.

The Computer Wings programme is a flexible, scheme that allows allowing Candidates to choose the module or modules which are most appropriate to their current or future roles.

Computer Wings provides a total programme solution, including registration, automated testing and certification, and supporting training materials.

For any further information visit www.computerwings.com

Scottish Qualifications Authority (SQA) endorsement

The Computer Wings qualification scheme is mapped to the UK National Occupational Standards (NOS) and is endorsed by the Scottish Qualifications Authority (SQA). The Computer Wings programme has been credit rated and levelled for the Scottish Credit Qualifications Framework (SCQF).

Diagram Maker has been officially designated as SCQF level 6 with 4 credit points. To see the SCQF level and credits for all other Computer Wings Modules visit http://www.computerwings. com/endorsements

Get certified

You now have your Computer Wings Course Book, which is designed to bring your skills to the next level. The next step is to prove your competencies by taking the Computer Wings certification test. Computer Wings is endorsed by the Scottish Qualifications Authority (SQA) www.sqa.co.uk, a world renowned awarding body.

Register for your test

To gain your Computer Wings certification you need to register for your test with a Computer Wings Authorised Centre.

Computer Wings certification tests are only available through Authorised Centres. For further information visit www.computerwings.com

Computer Wings overview

Computer Wings® is an exciting new computer skills training and certification programme. The programme consists of ten standalone modules which focus on the productivity skills required in today's rapidly changing economy.

The Computer Wings certification programme comprises the following modules:

Project Manager

Plan, resource, execute and manage mid-sized projects to deliver high quality, well defined, organised results on time and on budget.

Mail Manager

Communicate and collaborate more effectively by becoming proficient in the use of email software to manage organisational scheduling and communication.

Diagram Maker

Enhance effective business communication by using diagram tools and image editing applications to create diagrams, images and conceptual schemes.

Newsletter Publisher

Produce professional quality newsletters, brochures, eshots or leaflets to support marketing activity and organisational communications.

Presenter Pro

Enhance business communications by developing the skills to create and deliver attractive, persuasive, and audience focused presentations.

Web Creator

Create and maintain informative and user-friendly websites to support internal and external communications.

Web Optimiser

Develop Search Engine Optimisation (SEO) skills to support and improve websites to increase traffic, create more impact, and generate higher sales.

Web Analyser

Use web analysis tools to measure the appeal of a website, view the origin of visits and referrals, and generate reports about website activity.

IT TroubleShooter

Develop the IT administration skills required to deal with hardware, software, memory and network issues in small IT network environments.

IT GateKeeper

Recognise important software, hardware and network security considerations in order to protect small IT network environments.

Computer Wings benefits

The Computer Wings certification programme enables Candidate to develop their skills and confidently address computing applications relevant to their needs.

The Computer Wings certification programme delivers:

- A recognised and valuable qualification.

- Practical skills, competencies and knowledge.

- Awareness of good practice, efficient and productive use of applications.

- Confidence to produce effective and professional looking outputs.

- Improved returns on human and ICT investments.

- Validation of skills and knowledge as evidenced by certification.

- A match between candidate skills and organisational needs.

- Enhanced collaborative skills within an organisation.

- Improved productivity through more efficient use of office applications.

- Improved communication across the organisation.

Content validation

Q-Validus work with Subject Matter Experts (SME's) and renowned international awarding bodies and international partners, to develop and deliver Computer Wings, which reflects a comprehensive and recognised skills and knowledge standard.

Computer Wings Course Books are developed by SME's across the range of specialist domains.

Ongoing content validity of Computer Wings Syllabus standards definition is maintained by the Syllabus Expert Group (SEG) using the Q-Validus online Content Validation Database (CVD), a bespoke software tool for standards validation. Expert feedback and comment from around the world, in respect of Computer Wings Syllabus measuring points, is collated and recorded in the Content Validation Database. The current Computer Wings Syllabus Version is Syllabus Version 1.0. The ongoing standards validation process for Computer Wings supports the continuing applicability and relevance of Computer Wings.

Experts wishing to provide technical comments and feedback in relation to Computer Wings Course Books, or seeking to participate as experts in relation to the Computer Wings Syllabus standards definition, should contact: technical@computerwings.com

Computer Wings Diagram Maker overview

Computer Wings is an internationally recognised computer and ICT skills standard. Computer Wings training and certification programmes help Candidates work more effectively by developing computer and ICT skills that deliver valuable productivity benefits.

Computer Wings Diagram Maker is a certification in the area of drawing and image editing skills. The core product referenced in this Course Book version is Microsoft Visio 2007.

The Computer Wings Diagram Maker certification validates Candidate skill and knowledge in using drawing and image editing software to create and edit diagrams, illustrations and visual schemes in order to clearly communicate with clients and stakeholders.

Diagram Maker is designed to provide practical competence with the major features and functions of Microsoft Visio to enable Candidates create and edit diagrams and illustrations to effectively represent workflow, processes, the organisation, or projects.

Candidates shall:

✓ Develop the skills to produce professional, informative drawings and illustrations.

✓ Create diagrams, drawings and shapes.

✓ Zoom in, pan around drawings, and add drafting guidelines.

✓ Save drawings in different formats, compress files, output for the Web.

✓ Move, nudge shapes, resize proportionately.

✓ Rotate and flip shapes, group, ungroup shapes.

✓ Add colours, patterns to shapes.

✓ Connect shapes with static or dynamic connections.

✓ Add text to shapes, format text in shapes.

✓ Work with an image editor, resize, duplicate, and arrange images.

✓ Scan and save images, import images from other sources.

✓ Adjust image contrast, brightness and add different effects.

✓ Output to a printer or file.

✓ Be aware of copyright issues and applicable laws and guidelines.

Diagram Maker Syllabus

Category	Skill area	Ref.	Measuring point
3.1 DIAGRAMS	*3.1.1 Create*	3.1.1.1	Open a new drawing, or existing drawing.
		3.1.1.2	Create a drawing using a line, pencil or free drawing tool.
		3.1.1.3	Use a template as the basis for a drawing.
		3.1.1.4	Add a shape to a drawing.
		3.1.1.5	Add. remove a stencil shape.
	3.1.2 View	3.1.2.1	Navigate throughout a drawing.
		3.1.2.2	Add, delete, reorder pages in a drawing.
		3.1.2.3	Zoom in on a drawing.
		3.1.2.4	Pan around a drawing.
		3.1.2.5	Apply drafting guides to help work with elements in the drawing.
	3.1.3 Save	3.1.3.1	Save a drawing.
		3.1.3.2	Save a drawing in another file format.
		3.1.3.3	Compress a drawing.
		3.1.3.4	Choose suitable image files in terms of size and resolution, and recognise implications for publication via print or Web.
		3.1.3.5	Save a drawing as a template.
3.2 SHAPES	*3.2.1 Manipulate*	3.2.1.1	Move, nudge a shape.
		3.2.1.2	Resize a shape proportionately.
		3.2.1.3	Copy, paste a shape.
		3.2.1.4	Rotate, flip a shape.
		3.2.1.5	Delete a shape.
		3.2.1.6	Group, ungroup shapes.
		3.2.1.7	Add, remove shapes from a group.
	3.2.2 Format	3.2.2.1	Change shape line style.
		3.2.2.2	Add fill colour, pattern effects to a shape.
		3.2.2.3	Add shadow, or theme effects to a shape.
	3.2.3 Connect	3.2.3.1	Make a connection between shapes.
		3.2.3.2	Delete a connection between shapes.
		3.2.3.3	Connect shapes automatically.
		3.2.3.4	Make static or dynamic connections.
		3.2.3.5	Change the connection points between shapes.

Category	Skill area	Ref.	Measuring point
3.3 TEXT	*3.3.1 Insert*	3.3.1.1	Add text to a drawing.
		3.3.1.2	Edit text in a block.
		3.3.1.3	Copy, paste text in a block, or between text blocks.
		3.3.1.4	Move a text block.
		3.3.1.5	Resize a text block.
		3.3.1.6	Adjust alignment in a text black.
		3.3.17	Apply a numbered list, bulleted list in a text block.
	3.3.2 Format	3.3.2.1	Change the font size, colour of text.
		3.3.2.2	Change the style of text in a text block.
		3.3.2.3	Apply a different colour in a text box.
		3.3.2.4	Rotate text in a text box.
3.4 IMAGES	*3.4.1 Create*	3.4.1.1	Open an image editor.
		3.4.1.2	Create an image file.
		3.4.1.3	Save an image under a file name.
		3.4.1.4	Compress an image file, using a suitable compression technique.
		3.4.1.5	Zoom in, Zoom out.
		3.4.1.6	Close the image editor.
	3.4.2 Scan, Import	3.4.2.1	Scan and save an image.
		3.4.2.2	Import an image from a digital device.
		3.4.2.3	Import an image from an image library.
		3.4.2.4	Save an image from a web page.
	3.4.3 Manipulate	3.4.3.1	Select an image.
		3.4.3.2	Select part of an image.
		3.4.3.3	Resize an image, change its resolution.
		3.4.3.4	Rotate, duplicate an image.
		3.4.3.5	Arrange images in layers.
		3.4.3.6	Copy, move an image.
		3.4.3.7	Crop an image.

Category	Skill area	Ref.	Measuring point
3.5 ENHANCE	*3.5.1 Text*	3.5.1.1	Add text to an image.
		3.5.1.2	Change font style, size, colour.
		3.5.1.3	Copy, move, delete text.
		3.5.1.4	Align text.
	3.5.2 Colour	3.5.2.1	Apply different colours in the image.
		3.5.2.2	Set different opacity/transparency levels.
		3.5.2.3	Adjust brightness, contrast, hue.
		3.5.2.4	Apply different effects in an image.
3.6 DELIVER	*3.6.1 Output*	3.6.1.1	Add headers and footers to a drawing.
		3.6.1.2	Preview, check and proof that drawing, image and text outputs are readable and accessible, and make any changes where necessary.
		3.6.1.3	Choose basic print options, and print.
		3.6.1.4	Publish a drawing in XPS format.
	3.6.2 Laws & Guidelines	3.6.2.1	Recognise international accessibility standards: World Wide Web Consortium (W3C).
		3.6.2.2	Recognise the significance of disability/equality legislation in helping to provide all users with access to computers.
		3.6.2.3	Be aware of copyright laws and their impact for downloading content from the Internet, and in terms of image usage, and apportion due credit for use.
		3.6.2.4	Recognise house style guidelines and branding specifications.

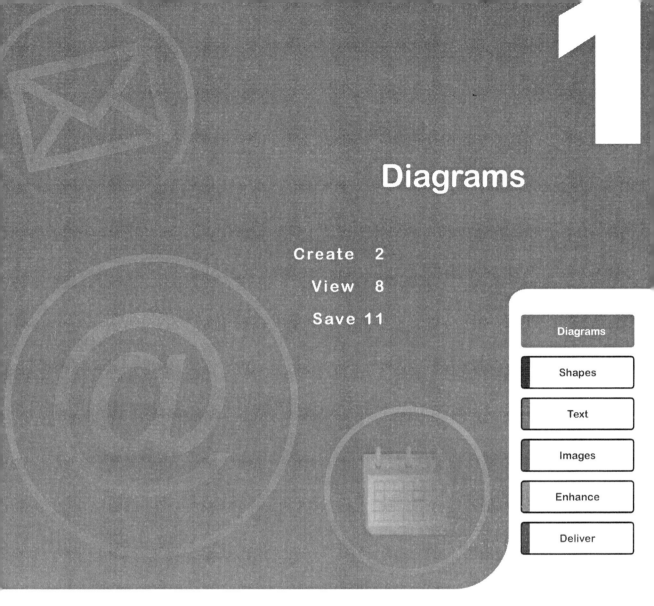

Diagrams

Create   2

View   8

Save   11

| Diagrams |
| Shapes |
| Text |
| Images |
| Enhance |
| Deliver |

Measuring points

- Open a new diagram, or existing drawing
- Create a drawing using a line, pencil or free drawing tool
- Use a template as the basis for a drawing
- Add a shape to a drawing
- Add, remove a stencil shape
- Navigate throughout a drawing
- Add, delete, reorder pages in a drawing
- Zoom in on a drawing
- Pan around a drawing

- Apply drafting guidelines to help work with elements in the drawing
- Save a drawing
- Save a drawing in another file format
- Compress a drawing
- Choose suitable image files in terms of size and resolution, and recognise implications for publication via print or Web
- Save a drawing as a template

Introduction

Working with Microsoft Visio 2007 allows you to easily create professional quality drawings and diagrams to help communicate, and share visual complex information such as systems, structures, and processes.

This chapter explains how Visio provides useful features to help you quickly create new drawings based on a comprehensive set of templates and various drawing tools. With Visio you can easily incorporate shapes representing objects and concepts in your drawings.

This chapter covers how to navigate between multiple pages in a drawing, adjust the view and focus to a particular area of your work, and how to save the drawing in different formats recognised by other software programmes. File compression is also dealt with in this chapter to facilitate easier file sharing with your work colleagues.

Create

Opening Visio

Creating quality diagrams with Visio templates allows you to illustrate complex business processes and data effectively and assist key decision making activities within your organisation. Visio provides a comprehensive range of template categories that incorporate many sample business data and work flow diagrams, organisation charts, electrical drawings, IT network diagrams, database modelling templates and much more to help you quickly create professional quality diagrams for all your business communication needs.

You can quickly add and arrange shapes, text, data and other graphical themes and effects in your diagrams to control and enhance their appearance and allow you visually communicate more effectively with your target audience.

Visio is available when you access your Microsoft Office applications. To open Visio:

1.   Open *Start* menu, select *All Programs*.

2.   Select *Microsoft Office* from the available programs menu.

3.   Select Microsoft Office Visio 2007.

4.   The *Setting Started with Microsoft Office* pane is displayed:

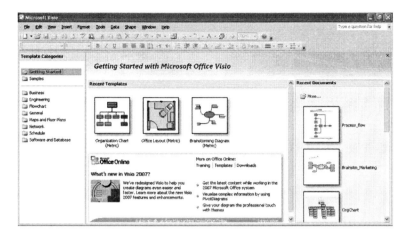

There are many ways in which commands can be carried out with different software products; menus, toolbar icons, a keyboard command, or a right-click can all be used. A visual approach is taken as the main task pathway for learning here; for example, making text bold could be achieved by using a toolbar icon or the keyboard shortcut: *Ctrl+B*. Candidates and Trainers should be aware that in this course book a menu or dialogue based approach is used as the preferred learning pathway.

Create a new drawing

To create a new drawing:

Actions

▶ 1. Select *File*, click *New*.

▶ 2. Select *New Drawing (Metric)*.

  Alternatively click the *New* icon on the toolbar.

  Or use the short cut key *Ctrl+N*.

A new drawing screen is displayed:

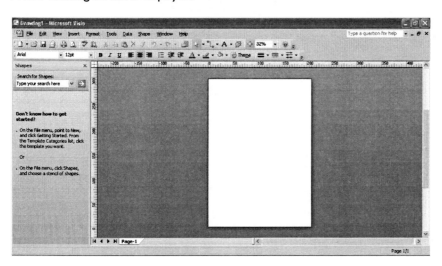

Using drawing tools

The *Drawing* toolbar contains various graphical tools that allow you to create shapes and focus in your drawings.

If the *Drawing* toolbar is not displayed do the following:

Actions

▶ 1. Click *View*.

▶ 2. Point to *Toolbars*, click *Drawing*.

Using templates

Visio incorporates a wide range of templates for your drawing requirements.

The following illustrates how to access and use a template in Visio, using a flow chart diagram for demonstration. To access and use a template in Visio:

Actions

▶ 1. Open *Visio*.

▶ 2. In the list of *Template Categories window* select *Business*.

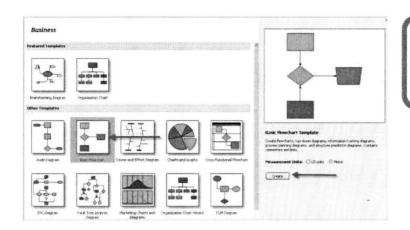

A drawing based on basic process flowchart template is displayed with some associated shapes. Different shapes are grouped into stencils in the *Shapes* pane to the left of the screen.

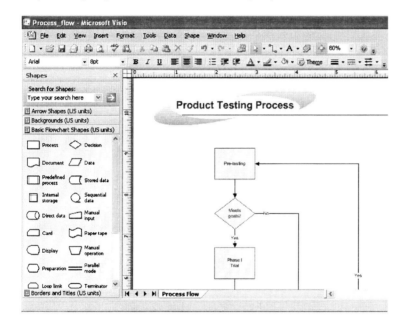

Saving a drawing as a template

To save a drawing as a template:

1. Click *File*.

2. Click *Save As*.

3. Enter a name for your drawing in the *File name* box.

4. Select file type and select *Template*.

5.   Choose a location to save your file.

6.   Click *Save*.

 In Visio, templates are displayed with a yellow border at the top of the template icon.

Adding shape

To add shapes to a drawing page:

1.   Click on a *stencil title bar,* (*arrow, shapes, backgrounds*, etc) in the left hand pane to see the shapes available on that stencil.

2.   Drag the required shape from the shapes on the left pane.

3.   Drop it onto the page at the appropriate position.

4.   Repeat steps 2 and 3 above to add more shapes to your drawing as necessary.

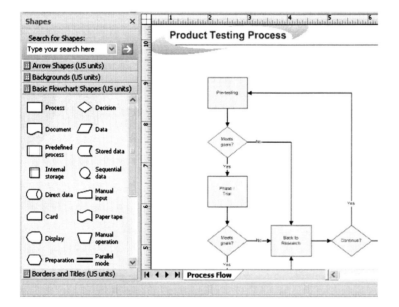

Using stencil shapes

Visio uses stencils to organise shapes so that you can easily find your required shape. A stencil is effectively a collection of related shapes associated with a Visio template. You can create your own stencil to organise shapes you use on a regular basis:

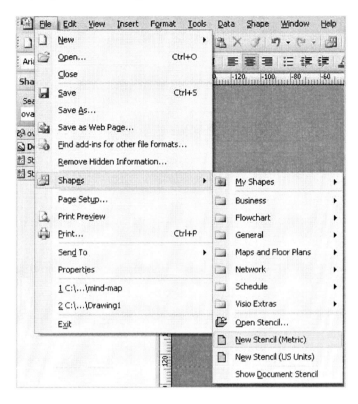

Action

▶ 1. Select *File*.

▶ 2. Point to *Shapes*, and click *New Stencil (Metric)*.

▶ 3. Right-click the *stencil title bar*, click *Save*.

▶ 4. Type a name for your new stencil, and click *Save*.

You can access the new stencil in the *Shapes* pane.

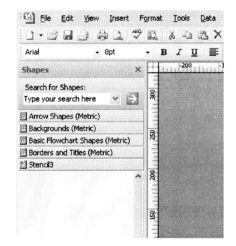

You can also enter text in the *Search for Shapes* box to search for particular shapes contained in other stencils.

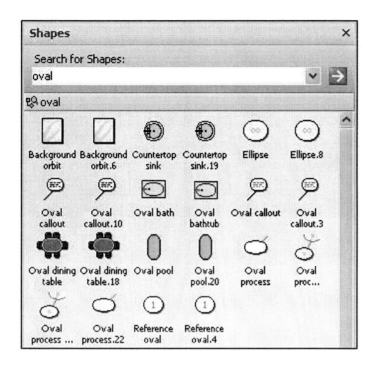

View

Accessing different pages

As you work in Visio, you can frequently have multiple pages in a drawing to maintain related diagrams or file revisions in the same file. To move quickly between these pages, click the required page tab in the bottom left area of the drawing window to access and view the required page of the drawing, as illustrated:

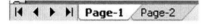

 To browse through pages in a drawing quickly, press *Ctrl+Page Down*, *Ctrl+Page Up*, or *Ctrl+Alt+Tab* as required.

Managing pages

You can right-click any page tab in your drawing to perform various page management tasks such as inserting, deleting pages, renaming and reordering pages.

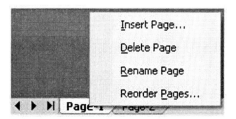

Actions

▶ 1. Right-click on any of the *page tabs* in your drawing.

▶ 2. Select the required menu option to *Insert*, *Delete*, *Rename* or *Reorder* pages.

Zoom

As you work in Visio, you can adjust your view of a drawing by changing the magnification setting to suit your requirements. This is a useful feature when creating complex drawings.

Depending on your display requirements, use the *Zoom* button in the *Standard* toolbar to adjust the page view as follows:

- Choose your required Zoom ratio by choosing a percentage display value.

- Select *Last* to reset the view to the previous percentage value specified.

- Select *Width* to view the full width of the drawing page.

- Select *Page* to view the entire drawing page.

 You can also click *View*, point to *Zoom* and select the required magnification settings.

Pan

To pan is to zoom in on a specific area of a drawing.

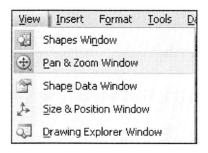

Actions

▶ 1. Click *View*.

▶ 2. Click *Pan & Zoom* Window.

The following screen is displayed:

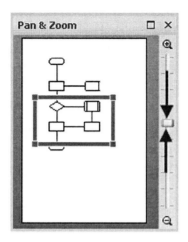

Displaying rulers, grids and guides

As you create drawings in Visio, it is good practice to display the vertical and horizontal rulers, gridlines and guides to help you visually position and measure elements and shapes in your drawing page.

A drawing window contains vertical and horizontal rulers that display measurement units at the scale of the drawing. When you move shapes in a drawing, faint lines display on the rulers to show the position of the shapes.

To display vertical and horizontal rulers in the drawing page, click *View* and then click *Rulers*.

You can also display gridlines in drawing page to help you position shapes visually. To display the grid on a drawing page, select *View* and then click *Grid*.

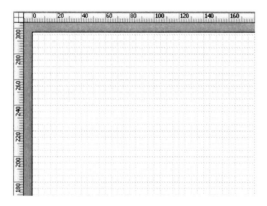

You can drag from any position in the vertical or horizontal rulers to add guides to your drawing page to help you visually position and align multiple shapes in your drawing. To display guides in the drawing page, click *View* and then click *Guides*.

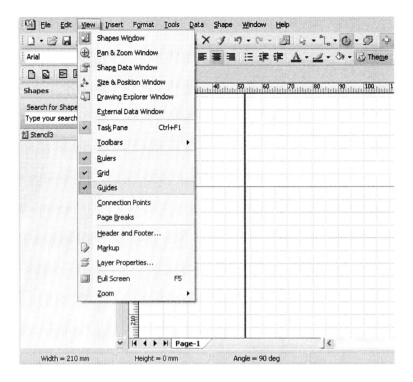

Save

Saving a drawing

To save a drawing in Visio:

1. Click *File*.

2. Select *Save As*.

3. Enter a name and choose a location for your file.

4. Click *Save*.

 The standard Visio drawing file extension format is used: .vsd.

Visio allows you to save a drawing in various formats recognised by other software applications.

You can save Visio drawing files in various file format including stencils and templates. Visio also allows you to save your drawings, stencils or templates in eXtensible Markup Language (XML) format, which is a standard format for sharing files between different software programmes. The various *Save* options are illustrated:

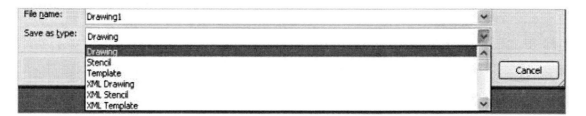

File compression

It is good practice to compress a Visio drawing file to reduce the total file size. This is particularly useful if you email Visio drawing files to your work colleagues for review. Visio drawings can quickly become large due to their graphical content.

To compress a drawing file saved to your desktop:

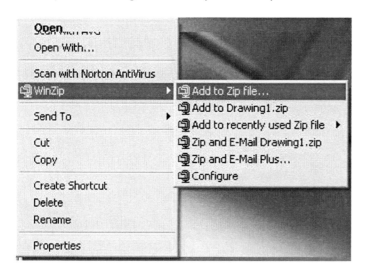

Actions

▸ 1. Right-click *WinZip*.

▸ 2. Click *Add to Zip file*.

▸ 3. Choose a name for the zip file and change the archive location if necessary.

▸ 4. Click *Add*, to compress the file into a WinZip file.

There are various compression utility tools available, WinZip is dealt with here. While other compression packages may differ slightly in their procedures the approach is very much the same.

Quick Quiz

Select the correct answer from the following multiple-choice questions:

1   What is Visio?

    a   An image manipulation program

    b   An organisational chart presentation tool

    c   A diagram and drawing package

    d   A template for drawing a basic flowchart

2   Which are the following is a collection of shapes in Visio?

    a   Palette

    b   Stencil

    c   Theme

    d   Protocol

3   What is a typical way to adjust your view of a drawing?

    a   Use the *Zoom* button on the *Standard* toolbar

    b   Drag the drawing to a different location

    c   Select the shape and click *Configure Layout*

    d   Select *View* and click *Task Pane*

4   Why is the XML format often used when saving a drawing?

    a   It is the only format supported by Visio

    b   It can be used to exchange data between systems

    c   It is a default file format

    d   It is used exclusively by Microsoft

5   How is a Visio drawing that is saved as a template distinguished from other Visio files?

    a   It has the word 'template' in the file name

    b   There is a red border around the icon

    c   There is a yellow border at the top of the icon

    d   The file extension is added

Answers to Quick Quiz

1   c   A diagram and drawing package

2   b   Stencils

3   a   Use the *Zoom* button on the *Standard* toolbar

4   b   It can be used to exchange data between system

5   c   There is a yellow border at the top of the icon

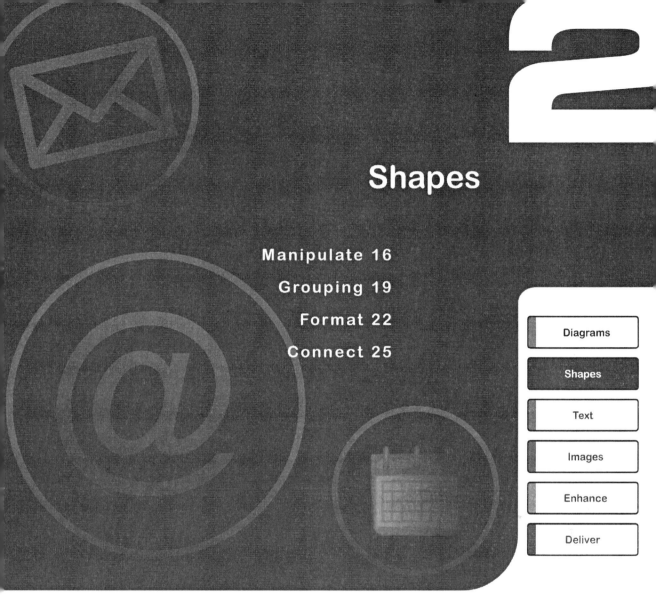

Shapes

Diagrams

Shapes

Text

Images

Enhance

Deliver

Measuring points

- Move, nudge a shape
- Resize a shape proportionately
- Copy, paste a shape
- Rotate, flip a shape
- Delete a shape
- Group, ungroup shapes
- Add, remove shapes from a group
- Change shape line style

- Add fill colour, pattern effects to a shape
- Add shadow, theme effects to a shape
- Make a connection between shapes
- Delete a connection between shapes
- Connect shapes automatically
- Make static or dynamic connections
- Change the connection points between shapes

Introduction

Working with Visio enables you to easily manipulate and manage shapes to assist in the design and creation of professional looking drawings that convey a strong visual and consistent design theme.

This chapter shows you how to position, resize, copy, rotate, delete shapes and change their orientation. It also describes how you can quickly group multiple shapes to change their format properties simultaneously or ungroup them to apply individual design formats as necessary.

This chapter also covers how to apply different line styles, change colour, pattern, fill and transparency formats for shapes, and apply shadow effects, theme colours and theme effects to achieve a more consistent visual appeal to your drawings. How you can use Visio to connect shapes in your drawings using various connection methods, is also covered.

Manipulate

Moving and nudging

When you place a shape in a drawing, you may subsequently need to move it to another location.

Moving a shape

To move a shape in a drawing:

1.   Open the required drawing in Visio.

2.   Click on the shape, green handles appear around the shape.

3.   Click on the dashed outline and drag the shape to move it to the required position.

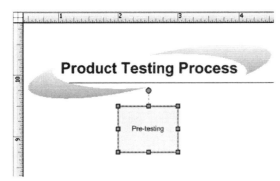

 To constrain the movement of the shapes to a vertical or horizontal direction hold down the *Shift* key while you drag the shapes to the required location.

Nudging a shape

Visio enables you to accurately nudge a shape to a precise position using the keyboard. The mouse is often less precise for shape manipulation. With the keyboard you can accurately position the shape. In the Workflow example illustrated, the arrow keys on the computer keyboard are used to accurately align the 'Meet goals?' shape to the 'Phase I trial' process shape.

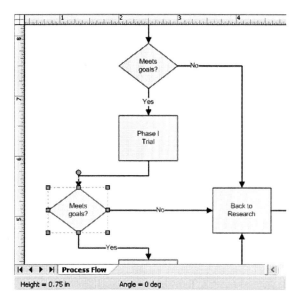

To nudge a shape into position select the shape you want to nudge and use the arrow keys to nudge it into position.

Resizing

To resize a shape maintaining its scale and proportion:

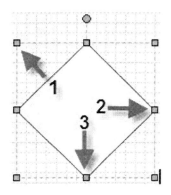

> ### Actions
>
> ▶ 1. Select the shape.
>
> ▶ 2. Choose a corner handle.
>
> ▶ 3. Click and drag the corner handle to resize the shape proportionately.

If you wish to change the dimensions of the shape, the non-corner handles can be used to adjust width and height.

Copying

You can save time where there are multiple instances of the same shape in the drawing page by copying and pasting the required shape as necessary.

Choose one of the following options to copy a shape in a drawing:

1. Select the shape you want to copy.

2. Select *Edit* on the *Standard* toolbar, click *Copy*.

3. Move the cursor to the required location.

4. Select *Edit* click *Paste*.

    (Other ways to do this are by clicking the *Copy* and *Paste* buttons on the toolbar or use the shortcuts *Ctrl+C* and *Ctrl+V*.)

Rotating shapes

Visio allows you to rotate a shape in a drawing page to achieve the correct orientation with respect to other shapes in the drawing. In the example illustrated, a process shape has been dragged or copied into the drawing page and is displaying the wrong orientation.

To rotate a shape by using menu selections, to correct its orientation, select the shape:

*   For clockwise rotation, click *Shape*, point to *Rotate or Flip* and then click *Rotate Right*.

*   For counter clockwise rotation, click *Shape*, point to *Rotate or Flip*, and then click *Rotate Left*.

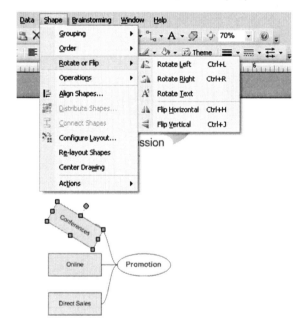

To rotate a shape using the rotation handle, select the shape:

- Click and drag a rotation handle in the required direction.

Flipping

Sometimes when creating drawings, you can locate a shape to use in your drawing but it faces in the wrong direction, you can flip the shape vertically or horizontally so it is facing in the required direction.

To flip a shape, select the shape and click *Shape*, point to *Rotate or Flip*, and then click *Flip Vertical* or *Flip Horizontal* as necessary.

Deleting

To delete a shape, select the shape and click *Delete* on the keyboard.

Grouping

You can manage multiple shapes in a Visio drawing page more effectively by grouping them temporarily as a single unit prior to performing common changes such as positioning, resizing, aligning, formatting or rotating. This beneficial practice saves you time and work effort by allowing you to simultaneously apply the same changes to multiple shapes in the Visio drawing page.

Grouping multiple shapes

To group multiple shapes in a drawing page:

1. Select all the shapes you want to group. This can be done using either of the following methods:

- Hold down *Shift* or *Ctrl* while clicking each shape in turn.
- Click the down arrow beside the pointer tool in Visio standard toolbar and click on the area you wish to select. Then click the pointer beside the shapes you want to select for grouping and drag around the shapes.

2. Click *Shape*, point to *Grouping* and click *Group*.

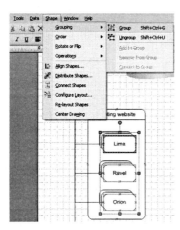

Ungrouping shapes

As you develop your drawing in Visio, you may want to ungroup a temporary group of shapes in your drawing page to quickly apply positioning or formatting changes to an individual shape and then the entire group of shapes.

To ungroup a group of shapes:

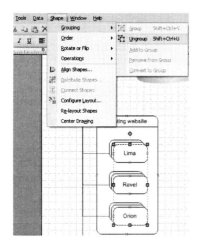

Actions

▶ 1. Select the required group into the drawing page.

▶ 2. Click *Shape,* point to *Grouping* and click *Ungroup.*

Adding a shape

To add a shape to a group:

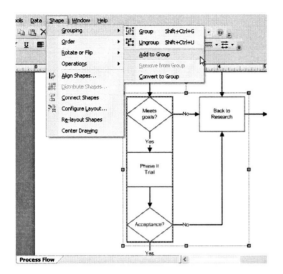

Actions

▶ 1. Select both the required shape and the group to which you want to add the shape.

▶ 2. Click *Shape*, point to *Grouping* and click *Add to Group*.

Removing a shape

To remove a shape from a group:

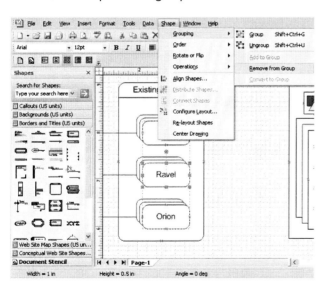

Actions

▶ 1. Select the group, and click the shape you want to remove from the group.

▶ 2. Click *Shape*, point to *Grouping* and click *Remove from Group*.

 When working with shapes in Visio, it is good practice to create a group of shapes on a temporary basis to quickly apply common changes such as positioning and formatting before you ungroup them again, (this is known as nested groups). Adding shapes to your drawing page and grouping them with another group of shapes causes the file size to increase significantly. This can impair Visio performance files.

Format

Changing a line style

You can apply a whole range of line formatting options such as colour, weight, pattern and transparency to visually enhance any shape outlines (normally a thin black line) in a drawing page.

To change the line style of a shape:

Actions

▶ 1. Select the required shape.

▶ 2. Select *Format* and then click *Line*. The *Line* diologue box is displayed.

▶ 3. Depending on your requirements, select any of the following line format options as necessary:

   • line pattern in the *Pattern* field.

   • line pattern in the *Weight* field.

   • line color in the *Color* field.

▶ 4. Change the line transparency, by moving the *Transparency* slider. Click a line style for the related shape.

▶ 5. Click *OK* to apply your changes.

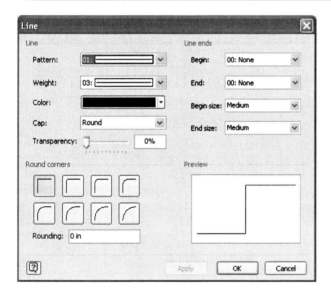

 To display the *Format Shape* toolbar, select *View*, click *Toolbar* and select *Format Shapes*.

Applying fill formatting to a shape

Visio provides a range of formatting options to fill a shape with a solid colour or with a pattern.

To apply fill formatting to a shape:

1. Select the required shape.

2. Select *Format* and then click *Fill*.

3. Depending on your requirements, click the *Fill* option you want and set at the level of transparency.

4. Click *OK* to apply your changes.

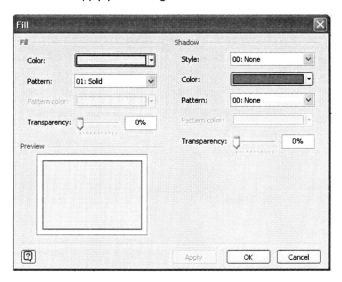

Applying a shadow

To apply shadow formatting to a shape

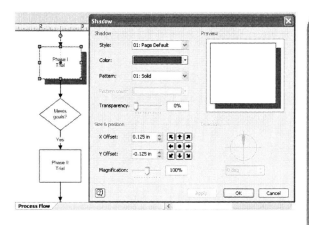

Actions

▸ 1. Select the required shape.

▸ 2. Click *Format* and then click *Shadow*.

▸ 3. Depending on your requirements click the *Shadow options* you want from the style, colour pattern and pattern colour links and set the level of transparancy.

▸ 4. To change the position of the shadow in relation to its shape (offset), insert a new value in the X offset.

▸ 5. Click *OK* to apply your changes.

Applying themes

Visio incorporates a comprehensive themes feature set that allows you to easily apply a professionally designed look to your drawings. A theme is a set of complementary colours and effects for fonts, fills, shadows, lines and connectors that you can mix and match in any combination to visually enhance your drawings and ensure design consistency.

To apply a theme:

1. Select *Format*.

2. Click *Theme*.

3. To display theme colours, in the *Theme* task pane, click *Theme Colours*.

4. To display theme effects, in the *Theme* task pane, click *Theme Effects*.

5. To apply a theme to the drawing page, right click a thumbnail and then click *Apply* to current.

6. To apply a theme to all the pages, right-click the required theme thumbnail, and then click *Apply to All Pages* on the shortcut menu.

Connect

Connecting shapes

You connect shapes in a drawing page to identify logical relationships between them. For example, to create an organisational chart in Visio, you need to use connector lines to show the reporting relationships between individuals and departments in an organisation. In the following organisation chart example, you want to show a reporting relationship between Nathan Randall (Engineering Director) and Margaret Brown (Research) using a connector line.

To show this reporting relationship using the *Connector* tool:

1. Click the *Connector tool* button 🔲 on the *Standard* toolbar.

2. Move the mouse over the Nathan Randall manager shape until it is highlighted by a red border.

3. Click and drag the mouse over the Margaret Brown position shape.

4. Release the mouse button and a connector line is displayed between both individuals.

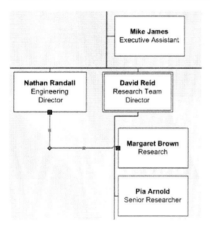

Manually

In the example illustrated, you want to show a reporting relationship from Nathan Randall (Engineering Director) to Joe Wilson (Assistant) and then show another reporting relationship from Joe Wilson (Assistant) to Emma Walsh (Junior Assistant). To manually connect these individuals in this order in the organisation chart:

1. Click the Nathan Randall manager shape first, then hold down the *Shift* key and click the Joe Wilson assistant shape followed by the Emma Wilson junior assistant shape to specify the connection order.

2. Click *Shape*.

3. Click *Connect Shapes* to connect these multiple shapes in the specified order.

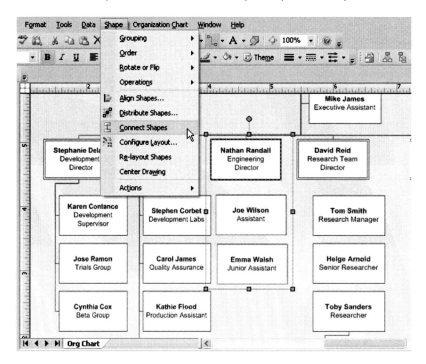

Automatically

To automatically connect:

1. Click the *Connector* tool on the *Standard* toolbar.

2. Add shapes to the drawing page. Each shape you drag from the stencil automatically connects to the shape previously added to the drawing.

Delete

If you find that you have added a connection unintentionally, and wish to delete it, apply the following actions:

1. Select the connector you want to delete.

2. Press *Delete* on the keyboard.

Creating connections

Static connections are fixed glue like connections between shapes, no matter where you move the shape the same connection points persist.

Dynamic connections will be re-drawn along the shortest path, when the shapes are moved.

Static

With static connections you want to have connection points that remain glued or connected to a specific point on a shape, even when one of the shapes is moved. In Visio, you can create connector lines using the *Connector* tool, which are called point-to-point or static connections.

In the following example, a static connection is created between a printer and a computer:

1. Click the *Connector* tool on the *Standard* toolbar, this acts as the 'glue' between the shapes.

2. Use the icon shown to apply the 'glue' between the shapes.

3. Move the mouse pointer over the connection point on the printer until it is highlighted by a red border.

4. Click and drag the mouse pointer over the target connection point on the computer until it is highlighted by a red border.

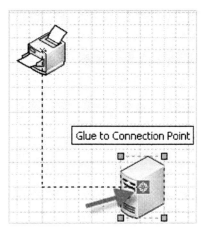

5. Release the mouse button and the static connection is created between the two selected connection points.

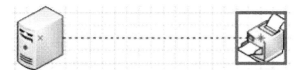

Dynamic

You can use the *Connector* tool in Visio to create shape-to-shape or dynamic connections between different shapes in your drawing. With a dynamic connection, the connector line remains glued to each shape by moving to the closest available connection points when you move either of the shapes. Dynamic connections are very useful for illustrating key relationships in Workflow diagrams, Gantt charts and conceptual illustrations.

In the following example, a dynamic connection is created:

1. Click the *Connector tool* on the *Standard* toolbar.

2. Move the mouse pointer over the shape until it is highlighted by a red border.

3. Click and drag the mouse pointer to connect to the other shape until it is highlighted by a red border.

4. Release the mouse button and the dynamic connection is created between the two shapes.

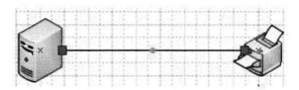

When the shapes are moved, the connector repositions so the two nearest points between the shapes are connected.

Changing connection points

If you need to change the connection point to which a connector line is attached or change the type of connection you can do this by disconnecting and reconnecting shapes:

To reattach shapes using a dynamic connection in a Visio drawing:

1. Drag the connector line end slightly away from the shape to disconnect it.

2. Drag the connector line back over the shapes centre to reconnect.

To reattach shapes using a static connection:

1. Drag the connector line end slightly away from the shape to disconnect it.

2. Drag the end connector line to a particular connection point to reconnect.

Quick Quiz

Select the correct answer from the following multiple-choice questions:

1   How do you 'nudge' shapes in Visio?

    a   By pressing *Ctrl+C*, then *Ctrl+V*

    b   By holding down *Shift* while you drag the shape

    c   By using the arrow keys on the keyboard

    d   By using the number keypad

2   What is the effect of 'grouping' shapes in Visio?

    a   You can treat them as one unit and so perform the same operation on them all

    b   You can save shapes more easily when they are in multiple groups

    c   Shapes become easier to rotate when they are grouped together

    d   Text can be added simultaneously when shapes are grouped

3   Why are 'themes' used in Visio?

    a   To give diagrams a particular appearance

    b   To make drawings more consistent and appealing

    c   To apply a unified set of design elements

    d   All of the above

4   What type of connection moves to a different connection point if you rearrange the shapes?

    a   A workflow connection

    b   A static connection

    c   A point-to-point connection

    d   A dynamic connection

Answers to Quick Quiz

1   c   By using the arrow keys on the keyboard

2   a   You can treat them as one unit and so perform the same operation on them all

3   d   All of the above

4   d   A dynamic connection

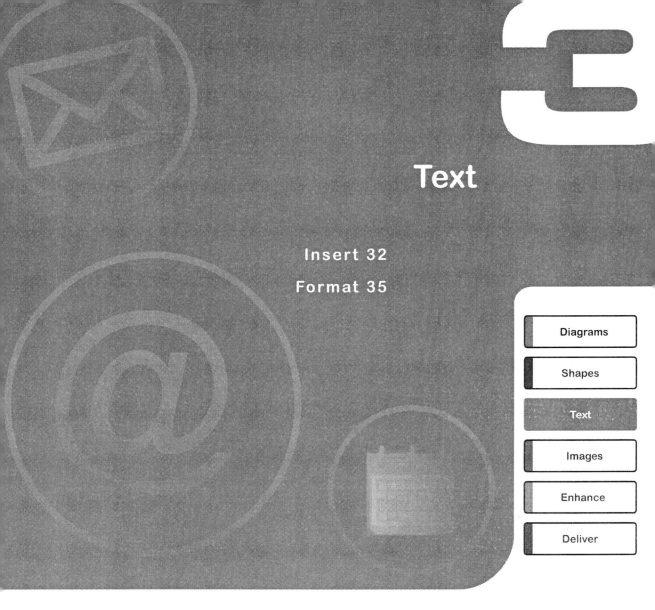

Text

Insert 32

Format 35

Diagrams

Shapes

Text

Images

Enhance

Deliver

Measuring points

- ▶ Add text to a drawing
- ▶ Edit text in a block
- ▶ Copy, paste text in a text block, or between text blocks
- ▶ Move a text block
- ▶ Resize a text block

- ▶ Adjust alignment in a text block
- ▶ Apply a numbered list, bulleted list in a text block
- ▶ Change the font size, colour of text
- ▶ Change the style of text in a text block
- ▶ Apply a different colour in a text box
- ▶ Rotate text in a text box

Introduction

When you add text in a Visio drawing, you can quickly format it using the extensive text styling features in Visio to highlight and communicate key areas visually.

This chapter explains how to add and edit text in a Visio drawing. It also explains how to move, resize and rotate text blocks, and adjust the text alignment. Applying different formatting options such as numbered and bulleted lists, font, style, size, case and colour settings to selected text in your drawing, is also covered.

Insert

Adding text

In Visio, you can easily add text that is independent of any shapes in your drawings to help bring clarity and focus to particular areas of your drawings. The easiest way to add text in a drawing is to activate or create a special frame called a text block that contains any text you type.

To add text to a drawing:

Action

▶ 1. Double-click any shape to activate its text block.

   Alternatively click the *Text Tool* icon on the toolbar. **A ·**

Actions

▶ 1. Type the required text.

▶ 2. Click outside the text block when finished.

Editing text in a text block

You may need to edit text previously added in a drawing as you develop concepts and schemes.

To edit text in a text block:

1. Double-click the shape to display the text.

2. Type your edited text as necessary.

3. Click outside the shape when finished.

Copying text

There are various options in Visio for copying text within drawings. You can choose key combinations in your computer bar, menu bar options or right-click menu commands.

To copy text using the *Standard* toolbar:

1. Double-click the text you wish to copy.

2. Click on the *Copy* icon on the *Standard* toolbar.

3. Click the shape where you want to copy the text.

4. Click on the *Paste* icon on the *Standard* toolbar.

The procedure described also applies for copying text within a text block.

Manipulate a text block

Visio has a full set of text manipulation features, allowing you to copy, move and align text insertions and make edits.

Moving

As you develop your drawings, you may need to move a text block independently of their shapes to a different location on your drawing page.

To move a text block:

1. Click the down arrow on the *Text Tool* icon on the toolbar. **A ·**

2. Click the *Text Block Tool* icon. Ⓒ

3. Click the shape that contains the text you want to move.

4. Position the *Text Block Tool* pointer over the text in the required text block and drag it to another location in the drawing page.

Resizing

To resize a text block proportionately:

1. Select the text block.

2. Choose a corner handle.

3. Click and drag the corner handle to resize the shape proportionately.

For height and width dimension changes, drag the side or bottom handle to make the adjustments.

Aligning

To change how text in a text box is aligned, ensure that the formatting toolbar is displayed. To do this click *View*, point to *Toolbars* and click *Formatting*. Select the text you want to align. Click the appropriate alignment button in the *Formatting* toolbar.

Creating a numbered list

You can create a numbered list in a text block drawing to indicate the order of importance and the order in which actions or steps occur.

To create a numbered list:

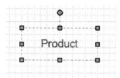 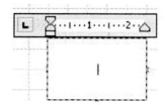

1. Select the text block.

2. Type the number for the first list item, press *Tab* key, type the text you want, and then press *Enter*.

   Repeat previous step for each numbered list item you want.

Creating a bulleted list

You can create a bulleted list in a text block in a drawing to highlight items in the text contents.

To change the bulleted style on selected text:

1. Select *Format*.

2. Click *Text*.

3. Click the *bullets* tab in the *Text* dialogue box.

4. Select the required bullet style or create a custom bullet list by inserting a new bullet character.

5. Click *OK*.

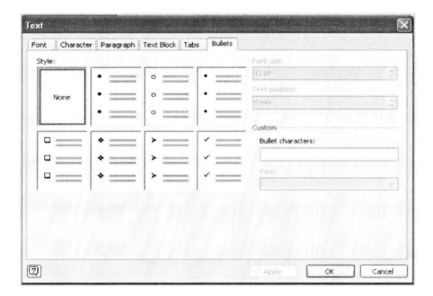

Format

Text formatting

At any stage, you can quickly apply all text formatting options as required for selected text in your drawing.

You can quickly format selected text or a text block to highlight or contrast it with adjacent text or other text blocks. Formatting options include applying different font, style, size, case and colour settings to selected text as necessary.

Text size and colour changes

To apply font size and colour formats to text in a drawing:

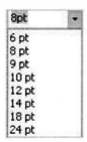

Actions

▶ 1. Select the required text in your drawing by double-clicking a shape to open it to text block.

▶ 2. Click the font size box in the *Formatting* toolbar and select a size.

▶ 3. Click the *Text Colour* button in the *Formatting* toolbar to change the colour of the text

Apply to all

At any stage, you can quickly apply all text formatting options as required to a selected text or a text block in your drawing.

To apply all formatting options to text in a drawing; select the required text.

1. Select text *Format*.

2. The *Text* box is displayed.

3. Depending on your requirements, you can select formatting options including font, size, case and column.

4. Click *OK* to apply your changes.

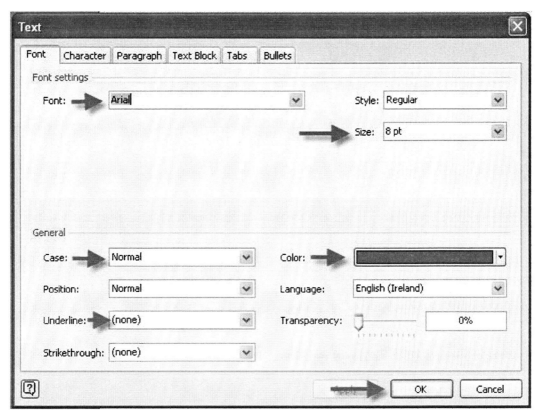

Rotating a text box

You can change the orientation of a text block by rotating it to set your drawing requirements:

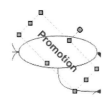

Actions

▶ 1. Click the *Text Block* icon.

▶ 2. Position the pointer over the rotating handle and drag as required.

▶ 3. As you drag the rotation handle, the pointer changes from a circular arrow.

▶ 4. Release at the required orientation.

Quick Quiz

Select the correct answer from the following multiple-choice questions:

1   What is the quickest way to change the appearance of text?

    a   By pressing *Ctrl+C*, then *Ctrl+V*

    b   Using the toolbar buttons

    c   By holding down the *Shift* key

    d   By using the arrow keys on the keyboard

2   How do you assess and display the text inside a square shape to enable editing?

    a   Use the *Zoom* option

    b   Copy the shape

    c   Double-click the shape

    d   Click on the shape corner

3   Where would you normally find the 'alignment' buttons?

    a   On the *Formatting* toolbar

    b   In the text box

    c   On the keyboard

    d   In the *Text* dialogue box

4   How would you change all of the features of a text box in one place?

    a   Use *Ctrl+Alt+P*

    b   Use *Format painter*

    c   Use the *Text* dialogue box

    d   Use Ctrl+Alt+G

5   What is a 'text block'?

    a   A set of instructions for removing connectors from a shape

    b   Text that has been copied from another source

    c   Something that prevents text being added to a shape

    d   A special frame for holding text

Answers to Quick Quiz

1 b Using the toolbar buttons

2 c Double-click the shape

3 a On the *Formatting* toolbar

4 c Use the *Text* dialogue box

5 d A special frame for holding text

Images

Diagrams

Shapes

Text

Images

Enhance

Deliver

Measuring points

▸ Open an image editor
▸ Create an image file
▸ Save an image under a file name
▸ Compress an image file, using a suitable compression technique
▸ Zoom in, Zoom out
▸ Close the image editor
▸ Scan and save an image
▸ Import an image from a digital device

▸ Import an image from an image library
▸ Save an image from a web page
▸ Select an image
▸ Select part of an image
▸ Resize an image, change its resolution
▸ Rotate, duplicate an image
▸ Arrange images in layers
▸ Copy, move an image
▸ Crop an image

Introduction

You can import a wide range of graphical image formats into Visio to visually enhance and identify or highlight particular areas of interest in your drawings.

This chapter explains how to use Microsoft Paint to save image files that you can import into Visio. It describes how you can compress an image file, scan and import an image from a digital camera into Visio, and save an image from a web page. This chapter also covers manipulating images by resizing, rotating and cropping them to change their appearance.

Create

Working with images

You can add different types of file images or graphics by importing them to create a new drawing or inserting them into an existing Visio drawing as necessary.

The following graphic file formats are supported by Visio:

- JPEG File Interchange Format (.jpg)

- Graphics Interchange Format (.gif)

- Portable Network Graphics (.png)

- Tag Image File Format (.tif, .tiff)

- Windows Bitmap (.bmp, .dib)

- Windows Metafile (.wmf)

- Enhanced Metafile (.emf)

- Compressed Enhanced Metafile (.emz)

- AutoCAD Drawing File Format (.dwg, .dxf)

- Scalable Vector Graphics Drawing (.svg, .svgz)

Opening an image editor

You can use a standard image edition such as Microsoft Paint to create and save graphic image files that you can subsequently use in your visio drawings.

To open an image editor:

1. Click *Start* on your desktop.

2. Select *All Programs*, click to *Accessories* and click *Paint*.

Saving an image file

To save an image file in Paint:

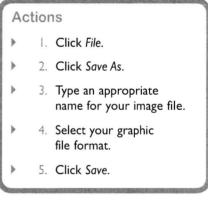

Actions

▶ 1. Click *File*.

▶ 2. Click *Save As*.

▶ 3. Type an appropriate name for your image file.

▶ 4. Select your graphic file format.

▶ 5. Click *Save*.

When you have finished working with your image file and you wish to close the image editor, click *File* and click *Exit*.

File compression

It is good practice to compress graphic image files to help reduce their size. This allows you to easily and quickly import image files into Visio for incorporation in your drawings.

To compress a file:

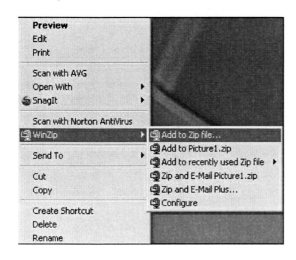

Actions

▶   1. Right-click the file on the desktop.

▶   2. Select *WinZip*.

▶   3. Select *Add to Zip file*.

▶   4. Confirm the file name and location.

▶   5. Click *Add*.

 Once the image file has been imported into Visio the image itself may also be compressed.

Zoom

Image editors have a range of viewing features that allow you to adjust zoom ratios and work effectively with images of different sizes and resolutions

To adjust the Zoom ratio of an image:

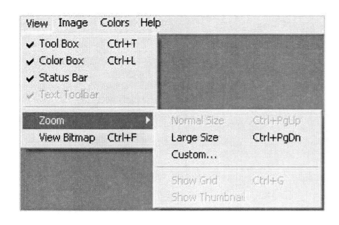

Actions

▶   1. While in Paint select *View*.

▶   2. Select *Zoom*.

▶   3. Choose a *Zoom* ratio or percentage value

Scan, Import

Adding images

Images from other sources such as scanned images, digital cameras, photo libraries or website images can all be used to enhance your work.

Scanning

You can use scanning software or an image editor installed on your computer to scan and import graphic image files.

To scan images:

1. Open the image editor or the scanning software.

2. Access the scanning device to display the image.

3. Select the parts of the image required.

4. Scan the image.

5. Save the image based on required image file formats. (Most scanners allow you to save for web or print quality formats).

 This scanning sequence is a standard approach, different image editors or scanning software may vary slightly in their procedures.

Digital camera

To import from a digital camera, start by attaching the camera to the computer and open the image editors. Select *File*, click *Open*, navigate to the appropriate device drive for the camera, access the relevant photo folder and open the required image. The image now displays in image editor.

Web

To save an image from a web page:

1. Right-click the image you want to save.

2. Select *Save Picture As*.

3. Choose a location for the file.

4. Click *Save in* required image format.

Manipulate

Handling images

In Visio, you can manipulate graphic image files in various ways to change their appearance and visually enhance particular elements or areas of your drawings. Depending on your graphical requirements, you can crop, resize, rotate, move and copy an image in your drawings as necessary.

Copying

To copy or move an image:

1.   Select the image.

2.   Right-click to select *Copy* or *Cut*.

3.   Move the cursor to the required location in your drawing.

4.   Right-click and select *Paste*.

Rotating

To rotate an image:

1.   Select the image by clicking on its rotation handle.

2.   To rotate the image, drag its rotation handle.

3.   Release the handle at the desired orientation.

Resizing

To resize an image while maintaining its scale and proportion:

1.   Select the image.

2.   Choose a corner handle.

3.   Click and drag the corner handle to resize the image proportionately.

 If you wish to change the dimensions of the image non-corner handles can be used to adjust width and height.

Cropping

Cropping involves trimming or removing the outer parts of an image to improve its framing and presentation.

To crop an image:

1. Click on the image to select it.

2. To display the picture toolbar select *View*, point to *Toolbars* and click *Picture*.

3. Click the *Crop* button.

4. Press down on one of the resizing handles and start to crop the image.

5. Drag the resize handle until only the area of the image you require is visible.

Quick Quiz

Select the correct answer from the following multiple-choice questions:

1   Which of the following are ways of importing information from other programs to Visio?

    a   Paste the information

    b   Insert the information

    c   Open another file type

    d   All of the above

2   What is Microsoft Paint an example of?

    a   A font colour

    b   A text block

    c   An image editor

    d   A static connection

3   What would you use to rotate an image?

    a   The *Rotation* handle

    b   The *Edit* menu

    c   A *Copy* button

    d   The *Scissors* command

4   What file type is a tif file?

    a   A text file

    b   An image file

    c   A compressed file

    d   A temporary file

Answers to Quick Quiz

1   d   All of the above

2   c   An image editor

3   a   The *Rotation* handle

4   b   An image file

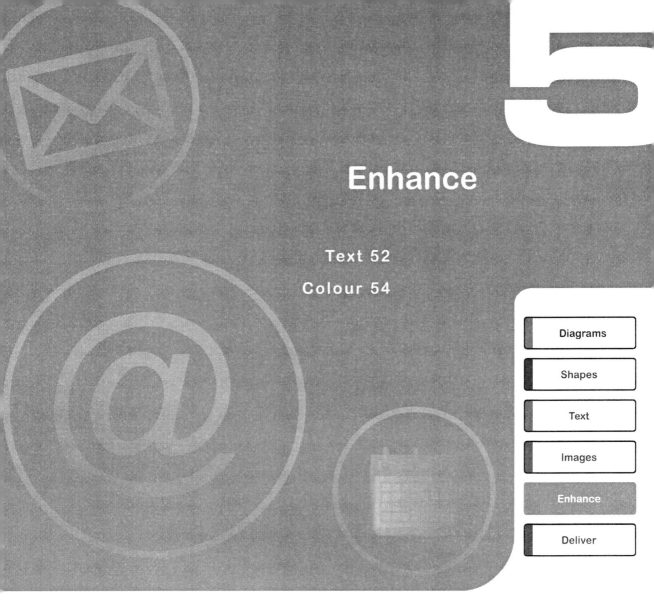

Enhance

Text 52

Colour 54

Diagrams

Shapes

Text

Images

Enhance

Deliver

Measuring points

- ▶ Add text to an image
- ▶ Change font style, size, colour
- ▶ Copy, move, delete text
- ▶ Align text

- ▶ Apply different colours in the image
- ▶ Set different opacity / transparency levels
- ▶ Adjust brightness, contrast, hue
- ▶ Apply different effects in an image

Introduction

You can draw audience attention to an image file in a Visio drawing by adding text to it and applying various text formatting options including, font, style, size and colour.

This chapter covers copying and moving text in a drawing and setting text alignment to suit your requirements.

This chapter also describes how you can significantly improve the display and print quality of an image in a drawing by specifying various image control settings such as brightness, contrast and transparency.

Text

Adding and formatting text

You can quickly add text to an image in a Visio drawing and apply various formatting options such as font, style, size and colour to generate visual interest in the text element of your image. In the illustrated example, some text is added to an image in a website drawing and various formatting options are applied to the text.

To add text:

1.   Open the drawing in Visio.

2.   Click the *Text Tool* on the *Standard* toolbar.

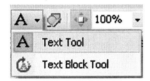

3.   Click and drag to create a text box beside the home page image in the drawing.

4.   Type the required text.

5. To apply formatting options, right-click the text, point to *Format* and click *Text*. The *Text* dialogue box is displayed; select the font style, size and colour required.

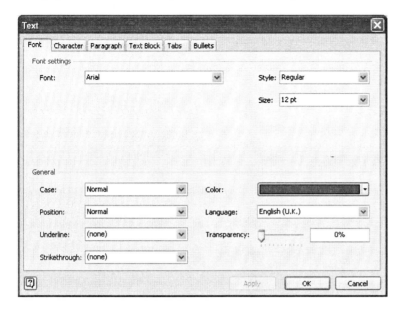

6. Click *OK* to apply the selected formatting options to the image text.

Copy, move or delete

To copy or move text:

1. Select the text you want to copy or move.

2. Click the *Copy* or *Cut* icon on the *Standard* toolbar.

3. Position your cursor into the required location in the drawing page.

4. Click the *Paste* icon on the *Standard* toolbar.

To delete text:

> **Actions**
>
> ▸ Select the text you want to delete.
>
> ▸ Click the *Delete* key on the keyboard.

Alignment

You can align text in different ways. To align text:

1. Right-click the text and click *Format* text.

2. Click the *Paragraph* tab in the Text box.

3. Under *Alignment* select an option.

4. Click *OK*.

You can also access alignment buttons on the *Formatting* toolbar.

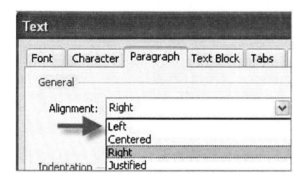

Colour

Working with colour

You can easily change the appearance of a graphic image file in a Visio drawing by adjusting various image effects such as contrast, brightness and transparency as necessary.

Contrast, brightness

Contrast is the distinction between colour and light in images.

To adjust the contrast and brightness for an image:

1. Right-click the image, point to *Format* and click *Picture*. The *Format Picture dialogue* box is displayed.

2. Click *Image Control*.

3. Drag the *Brightness* slider to the required setting or type a percentage value in the corresponding box. Choose a higher percentage to increase the colour brightness of the picture or set a lower percentage to achieve a darker picture colour as necessary.

4. Drag the *Contrast* slider to the required setting or type a percentage value in the corresponding box. Choose a higher percentage to increase the colour intensity in the picture or set a lower percentage to reduce the colour intensity as necessary.

5. Click *OK* to apply your changes to the image.

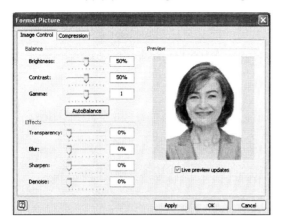

Transparency

To adjust the transparency for an image:

1. Right-click the image, point to *Format* and click *Picture*. The *Format Picture* dialogue box is displayed.

2. Drag the *Transparency* slider to the required setting or type a percentage value in the corresponding box. Choose a higher percentage to increase the transparency level of the picture or set a lower percentage to reduce the transparency level as necessary.

3. Click *OK* to apply your changes to the image.

 You can also specify other picture control settings such as *Gamma*, *Blur*, and *Sharpen* levels for the selected image.

Compression

The compression feature helps you work more efficiently with images and choose resolutions that best suit web or print outputs. The compression feature also allows you to remove cropped portions of an image, which are retained otherwise. To compress an image file, select the *Format Picture* dialogue box, select the *Compression* tab and choose the appropriate ratio.

Quick Quiz

Select the correct answer from the following multiple-choice questions:

1   To add text to an existing image the first action is to:

   a   Begin typing the text

   b   Copy the text from another source

   c   Double-click on the image

   d   Right-click on the text

2   How would you activate a pop-up menu that would allow you to format text?

   a   Right-click on the text

   b   Click the *Paste* icon

   c   It cannot be changed in Visio

   d   Delete the text and place it somewhere else

3   Which dialogue box allows you to adjust transparency levels?

   a   *Text*

   b   *Paragraph*

   c   *Format Picture*

   d   *Alignment*

4   Which term expresses the distinction between colour and light in an image?

   a   Brightness

   b   Contrast

   c   Transparency

   d   Hue

Answers to Quick Quiz

1 c Double-click on the image

2 a Right-click on the text

3 c *Text*

4 b Contrast

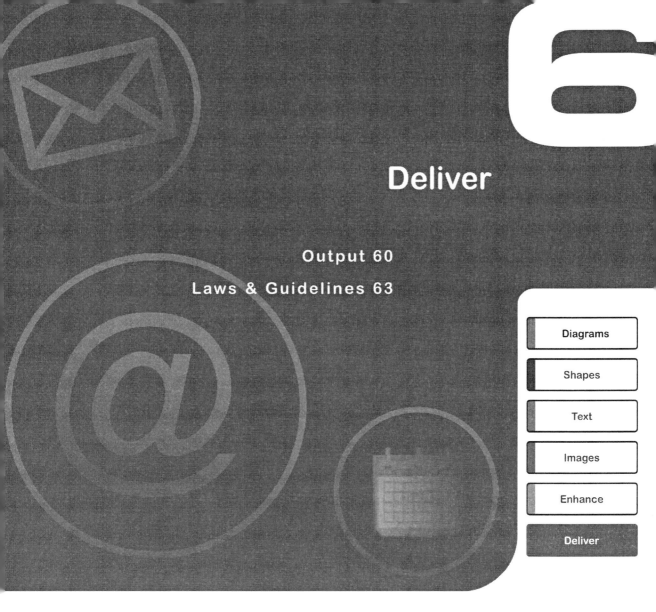

Deliver

Output 60

Laws & Guidelines 63

Diagrams

Shapes

Text

Images

Enhance

Deliver

Measuring points

- Add headers and footers to a drawing
- Preview, check and proof that drawing, image and text outputs are readable and accessible, and make changes where necessary
- Choose basic print options, and print
- Publish a drawing in XPS format
- Recognise international accessibility standards: World Wide Web Consortium (W3C)

- Recognise the significance of disability / equality legislation in helping to provide all users with access to computers
- Be aware of copyright laws and their impact for downloading content from the Internet, and in terms of image usage, and apportion due credit for use
- Recognise house style guidelines and branding specifications

59

Introduction

Using Visio allows you to customise your drawing files through the incorporation of header and footer content such as automatic page numbering, filenames and revision dates.

This chapter describes how to preview the content of your drawing files prior to publication for visual integrity and legibility. It also covers how to specify different print options, print your drawings and publish them in XPS format for sharing in a collaborative work environment.

Output

Adding headers and footers

Prior to printing you may wish to add header or footer information to your drawing. You can add different types of information to the headers and footers of your Visio drawings to generate professional quality printed documentation. Such information can include company name and logo, page numbers, current date and time, and filenames.

In the illustrated example, header and footer information is added to a Workflow chart:

1. Open the *Workflow* chart in Visio.

2. Click *View*.

3. Click *Header and Footer*. The *Header and Footer* dialogue box is displayed.

4. Fill in the required information in the *Header* and *Footer* fields, such as 'Test workflow chart'.

5. By clicking on the arrows on the right of each field, a whole range of default entries are given in a drop-down list, as 'Current date'.

6. Click *OK*. Note that your header and footer information is displayed when you print the Workflow chart.

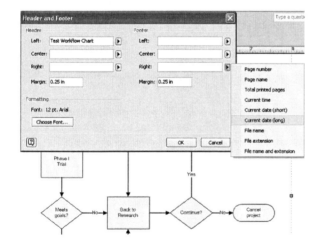

Preview

Prior to printing your Visio drawings, it is good practice to check them visually when completed to determine that there will be no viewing or printing problems such as the misplacement of shapes with respect to the drawing page margins or drawings exceeding the specified page size.

You can use the *Print Preview* feature in Visio to preview your drawing for visual integrity and legibility and make any necessary page setup adjustments to ensure it prints correctly.

To preview a Visio drawing prior to printing:

1. Click *File*.

2. Click *Print Preview*.

3. Click the *Setup* button. The *Page Setup* dialogue box is displayed.

4. Make any necessary adjustments by clicking the *Print Setup*, *Page Size*, *Drawing Scale* and *Page Properties* tabs as required.

5. Click *OK* to apply the changes.

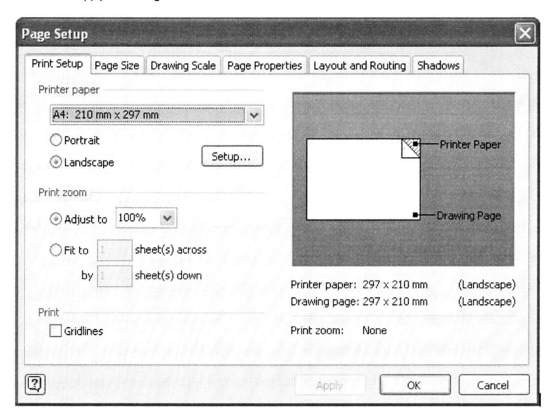

Setting print options

To set print options for your drawings:

1. Click *File*.

2. Click *Print*.

3. The *Print* dialogue box is displayed.

4. Specify the *Printer* and *Page Range* options as required, such as *number of copies* etc.

5. Click *OK* to print the drawing.

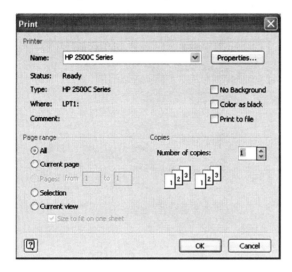

Publishing a drawing in XPS format

You can save or publish a Visio drawing file in XML Paper Specification (XPS) format if you have already installed the Save as PDF or XPS plug-in for Microsoft Office 2007. The XPS file allows you to safely share your Visio drawing files and maintain all source diagram formatting that cannot be modified when viewed online.

 Note that you must download a free XPS viewer from Microsoft (visit www.microsoft.com) in order to display XPS files on your computer.

To publish a Visio file in XPS format:

1. Open the required Visio drawing.

2. Click *File*.

3. Click *Publish as PDF* or *XPS*, the *Publish as PDF* or *XPS* dialogue box is displayed.

4. Type a file name for the drawing and select XPS Document from the *Save as type* list.

5. Depending on your publishing requirements, choose one of the following options:

    - For professional print quality, click *Standard* (for printing and publishing online).
    - For optimum file size, click *Minimum* size (publishing online).

6. Click *Options* and specify various print options such as printing the current page, all pages in the drawing, or a range of pages.

7. Click *OK* to confirm your publishing selections.

8. Click *Publish*.

Law & Guidelines

World Wide Web Consortium (W3C)

The World Wide Web Consortium (W3C) is an international consortium whose member organisations work together to develop Web standards for the purpose of making the Web accessible to all users. It was established in 1994 as a collaboration between the Massachusetts Institute of Technology (MIT) and the European Organisation for Nuclear Research (CERN) and today has 400 members, including the likes of Microsoft, IBM, Apple, Sun Microsystems as well as telecommunications companies, standards bodies, academic institutions and research centres.

W3C's most important work is in the development of Web specifications or standards ('Recommendations') that describe communication protocols, such as HTML and XML, and other building blocks of the Web. Since its inception W3C has published more than 110 such standards or W3C Recommendations with the goal of ensuring compatibility between Web technologies so that the Web can reach its full potential by allowing hardware and software used to access the Web to work together.

Disability / equality legislation

Disability legislation prohibits direct discrimination, victimisation and harassment and promotes equality for disabled people. Disability legislation, in particular, makes it unlawful to discriminate against people in respect of their disabilities in relation to such matters as employment, the provision of goods and services, education and transport.

At national level, policies relating to people with disabilities reflect the diversity of cultures and legislative frameworks in the EU Member States: the definitions and the criteria for determining disability are currently laid down in national legislation and administrative practices and differ across the current Member States according to their perceptions of, and approaches to, disability.

You should be aware of your own applicable national legislation as well as relevant international directives.

Copyright and the Internet

Copyright material published on the Internet will generally be protected in the same way as material in other media. Copyright is protected internationally through international treaties, such as, the Berne Convention to which over 160 countries are parties to. Before the Berne Convention, national copyright laws usually only applied for works created within each country.

Copyright has two main purposes, namely the protection of the author's right to obtain commercial benefit from valuable work and the protection of the author's general right to control how a work is used. Almost all works are copyrighted the moment they are written and no copyright notice is required.

You should be aware that if publishing material from other sources the express permission of the copyright owner (unless copyright exceptions apply) is required. In all cases, copies should be acknowledged as far as is practical. In addition, many websites will include a copyright statement setting out exactly the way in which materials on the site may be used.

You should also be aware that many online resources may have been published illegally without the permission of the copyright owners. Any subsequent use of the materials, such as printing, or copying and pasting, may also be illegal.

For further details on copyright requirements within your own country please refer to your own applicable national legislation.

Quick Quiz

Select the correct answer from the following multiple-choice questions:

1   Which menu allows access to headers and footers?

    a   *View*

    b   *Format*

    c   *Tools*

    d   *Shape*

2   Which of the following is a good reason to always preview your drawings?

    a   You cannot print until you have previewed a drawing

    b   To make sure that the drawing displays within the borders page

    c   To check that a printer is connected

    d   So you can save your drawing as a web page

3   Which of the following may be a valid course of action if your drawing falls across a number of pages?

    a   Print on larger paper

    b   Adjust the placement of the shapes

    c   Reduce the size of the drawing

    d   All of the above

4   What is the name of the authoring language used to create documents on the Web?

    a   CSS

    b   URL

    c   HTML

    d   W3C

Answers to Quick Quiz

1   a   *View*

2   b   To make sure that the drawing displays within the page borders

3   d   All of the above

4   c   HTML